Published by
Stanley R. Abbott Ministries, Inc.
P.O. Box 533
McRae, Georgia 31055
U.S.A.

The Church

PREFACE

I remember the powerful testimony of the late John Wimber, founder of Vineyard Ministries, and former manager of The Righteous Brothers, a popular singing duo in the 1950's. As the story goes, right after John's acceptance of Jesus as Lord, he attended a church service one Sunday morning. At the conclusion of the service John went up to the Pastor with his Bible open and asked the Pastor when they were going to do the *"...stuff..."*. The Pastor asked, *"...what stuff..."*, to which John replied, *"...the stuff here in the Bible..."*, referring to the works of Christ. The Pastor gave John a traditional answer, but John did not receive it as truth, and Vineyard Ministries sprang up from the seed of John Wimber's refusal to accept tradition and the doctrine of man as a substitute for the revelation of Christ.

Every single person who is born again partakes of the nature of their heavenly Father, just like every single person who is born into this natural world partakes of the nature of their earthly father.

> *"He came to His own, and His own did not receive Him. But as many as received Him, to them He gave the right to become children of God, to those who believe in His name; who were born, not of blood, nor of the will of the flesh, nor of the will of man, but of God."* **John 1:11-13**

This divine nature creates a longing for the things of God. The newly born again babe in Christ has an innate hunger for

God. The only way this hunger can be satisfied is by partaking of the knowledge of God, revelation from heaven. The only way this hunger will go away is for the believer to forsake continuing in the word and being a doer, and replacing it with something else.

Hunger for God can be revived if the believer will simply turn his heart back toward the Lord. John exiled on the isle of Patmos recorded the words Jesus gave him for the church at Laodicea. The believers at Laodicea had shut Jesus out of the practice of their lives. Jesus wanted them to see how corrupt their lives had become. In this context He instructed John to write these words for the Laodiceans...

> *"...Because you say, 'I am rich, have become wealthy, and have need of nothing' and do not know that you are wretched, miserable, poor, blind, and naked; I counsel you to buy from Me gold refined in the fire, that you may be rich; and white garments, that you may be clothed, that the shame of your nakedness may not be revealed; and anoint your eyes with eye salve, that you may see. As many as I love, I rebuke and chasten. Therefore be zealous ad repent. Behold, I stand at the door and knock. If anyone hears My voice and opens the door, I will come in to him and dine with him, and he with Me..."*
> **Revelation 3:20**

If you have lost your hunger for God, or worse if you were never hungry for God, then allow Jesus to enter your life so you may be filled. Turn your heart toward the Lord so you may hear His knock at the door of your heart.

He is knocking, can you hear it?

Table of Contents

The Church

Chapter One

THE EXPECTATIONS
OF CHRIST

"For I say, through the grace given to me,
to everyone who is among you,
not to think of himself more highly than he ought to think,
but to think soberly,
as God has dealt to each one a measure of faith..."
Romans 12:3

If we use the Bible as the written standard by which we *"...think soberly..."* of ourselves, it should be fairly easy to measure our lives according to the expectations of Christ. This measuring process must be applied to each of our individual lives and to our corporate identity; to our corporate identity on the local level and on the universal level. While much could be written about the expectations of Christ for each individual believer, only one expectation will serve our purpose for this book.

"Most assuredly, I (Jesus) say to you, he who believes in Me, the works that I do he will do also; and greater works than these he will do, because I go to My Father."
John 14:12

We surely can agree as to whether or not believers, or any measurable percentage of them, are doing the works of Jesus. According to **John 14:12**, they are not... The primary purpose of this book is to focus on Christ's expectations for the corporate church:

1

The Church

➤ *Where we are in relation to His expectations?*

➤ *Where we need to go to meet His expectations?*

➤ *How to get there?*

Division within the house of the Lord is **anathema** to our God! Unity is so important that in the midst of Jesus' communion with the Father just prior to His arrest, in the presence of His disciples, He prayed:

> *"As You sent Me into the world, I also have sent them into the world. And for their sakes I sanctify Myself, that they also may be sanctified by the truth. I do not pray for these alone, but also for those who will believe in Me through their word; that they all may be one, as You, Father, are in Me, and I in You; that they also may be one in Us, that the world may believe that You sent Me. And the glory which You gave Me I have given them, that they may be one just as We are one: I in them, and You in Me; that they may be made perfect in one, and that the world may know that You have sent Me, and have loved them as You have loved Me..."*
>
> **John 17:18-23**

This unity of which Jesus spoke is not just so we may be one, but for three other significant reasons:

1) *"...that the world may believe that the Father sent Jesus into the world...",*

2) *"...so that we may be made perfect...",*

3) *"...that the world may know the Father loves us just as He loves Christ...".*

It is easy to see why the enemy has targeted our unity!

2

We already know that *anything* divided cannot stand. Now, our understanding of division is broadening as we see that if the enemy can divide the church, it will greatly hinder the world from believing that the Father sent Jesus into the world and our goal of being complete or perfect. No wonder division is so rampant in the church in the earth. The enemy does not want the church to stand, but he also does not want the world to accept Jesus or for us to reach our complete state. The church in the earth is divided in part because we do not understand division, and because we do not see how destructive it is to the plans and purposes of God for us.

In Paul's first letter to the church at Corinth, he began to address the issues of division working among them. The scope of these devices was staggering. It touched almost every area of life in the church. Almost immediately after greeting the saints Paul began to plead with them. This action has always baffled me. Why does this great apostle of God plead with those whom he oversees? While there may be multiple answers to this question, the most palatable to my heart is the great love Paul had as a spiritual father to these believers. He wanted them to see his broken heart toward them as a result of their division. We know this apostle was extremely capable of rebuking the church sharply, but it is so comforting to my heart to think of him pleading with those he loved.

"Now I plead with you, brethren, by the name of our Lord Jesus Christ, that you all speak the same thing, and that there be no divisions among you, but that you be perfectly joined together in the same mind and in the same judgment." **I Corinthians 1:10**

What tenderness! What compassion! What care! What fatherly connection with his sons...

Throughout more than 30 years in ministry, most of it imparting apostolic revelation, a destructive cycle repeated itself over and over again in my life and ministry. I would become frustrated with people who did not seem to have their hearts turned toward the Lord. I would allow my frustration to turn to anger and ultimately into bitterness. Experiencing the consequences of this destructive cycle, but not really understanding its components, I would cry out to the Lord for help. The graciousness of our God would give me help through the tender ministry of the Holy Spirit, and I would find relief but never real deliverance from the root causing the cycle.

While overseeing a local assembly in the middle of 2012, the Lord Jesus took me by the hand and ushered me into a new level in the spirit. He told me very clearly this was a promotion, but that what had worked in previous levels would not work in this new level. He said He was requiring me to learn a new way! I had no idea what a revolution this was going to be in my personal life and ministry.

The main root causing the destructive cycle to continually repeat itself in my life and ministry was a false perspective of value. I had lived most of the entirety of my life with the false perspective that performance established value. Oh, how destructive this device was! We are valuable to our God because of who we are to Him, not as a result of what we do for Him. What we do is of vital importance; it just does not establish our value, just like Adam never lost his value to God because of what he did, but what he did cost him his place in the Garden. Scripture is so clear that even when we were dead in our sins God so loved us that He sent His only begotten Son to die for us. Scripture is also so clear that a person yielding to sin is taken captive by the enemy. Such a person remains valuable to God, even in his sin, but being a captive of the enemy is not a good thing!

If this false perspective is alive in a minister, there is absolutely no way that minister can value the sons of God appropriately. If the sons do not grow spiritually, he will see them as not valuable. If they do not have works accompanying their faith, he will see them without value. If the sons do not walk spiritually minded as a way of life, he will see them as less than. If they have any other performance based condition that is contrary to the will of God, and a spiritual father has the false perspective of performance establishing value, the enemy will rule in their relationship.

Once the Holy Spirit identified this root in me, it took months before I could finally be free from it. At the beginning of 2013 I was instructed to resign all roles in the local assembly I had overseen and return to the ministry of my beginning: *...training national Christian leaders...* and *...helping lay foundation...* in God's people everywhere. I am so confident deliverance from this root released me to return to my true apostolic purpose: **Ministry to the Nations!**

The subtle craftiness of the enemy and his devices have brought so much harm to the church. We have been so ignorant of his devices. They are more subtle and more aggressive than we ever imagined. However, we are beginning to awaken to them and find ways to overcome them. Not only being free from them, but being unhindered to do our Father's will is to be our priority. We must rid the church of division in any form.

As Paul, this tender hearted apostle, continued to write his letter to the church whom he loved so much, he addressed the issues of division among them. In what we have marked as chapter three Paul identifies yet another aspect of the results of division.

> *"And I, brethren, could not speak to you as to spiritual people but as to carnal, as to babes in Christ. I fed you with milk and not with solid food; for until now you were not able to receive it, and even now you are still not able: for you are still carnal. For where there are envy, strife, and divisions among you, are you not carnal and behaving like mere men? For when one says, "I am of Paul," and another, "I am of Apollos," are you not carnal?..."* **I Corinthians 3:1-4**

Paul could not fulfill his apostolic ministry to the church as spiritual people, which was his role and his responsibility assigned to him by God, because of their carnal condition which included *divisions* among them.

In precisely the same way that the awesome power of God was limited from working many mighty works through Jesus as Matthew recorded,

> *"Now He did not do many mighty works there because of their unbelief."* **Matthew 13:58**

...the apostolic anointing was limited from flowing to the church at Corinth because of the division among them. Division will stop or greatly hinder the anointing of God from producing the desired results God intends for His people. We must see this and defeat division in the church.

The Expectations of Christ

Where we are in relation to His expectations?

Firstly, "...the church is divided..."

If we use what we have read in the first few chapters of Paul's letter to the church at Corinth to compare their condition to that of the church in the earth today, the comparison is frightening. Paul identified the believers at Corinth as carnal and divided because of the way they identified themselves with various ministers. They were actually allowing division to occur among themselves on the basis of their identification with different ministers through whom they had received ministry.

The denominationalism dividing the church today is identical to what was happening in Corinth. Each modern day denomination represents the influence of typically a single minister who brought revelation to the people. In some instances the identification with the "...founding..." minister is disguised so the founder's name does not appear over the denomination. In other instances no such disguise exists. The denomination is simply identified by the founding minister's name followed by the letters -ian, or -an, or similar. In Bible times there were persons who followed King Herod; the way he dressed, the way he thought, the way he lived. These followers of Herod were called Herodians. It was clear by their name and their lifestyle who they were following.

Even if the believers at Corinth were using the name of Christ as a source of division from other believers, Paul identified this as a source of unhealthy division.

> *"For it has been declared to me concerning you, my brethren, by those of Chloe's household, that there are contentions among you. Now I say this, that each of you says, "I am of Paul," or "I am of Apollos," or "I am of Cephas," or "I am of Christ." Is Christ divided? Was Paul crucified for you? Or were you baptized in the name of Paul?"* **1 Corinthians 1:11-13**

Paul's motive to address these issues of division among the church was to help them see the insidious device of the enemy at work among them. Paul's paternal care for the church was without question. He was trying to awaken them to the door they had opened to the enemy by seeing themselves as mere men. No man will win against the enemy if that man sees himself only as a mere man. The only way we can win against this evil enemy is to see ourselves as spiritual men able to fight in the power God Himself has given us.

Perhaps a minister with a root of performance-establishes-value could possibly want to expose the division that exists in the church today with a lesser motive than simply loving the people and wanting them to go free. However, once this root and the consequences of division are identified, the minister's only motive will be to see the sons of God free from the bondages for which Jesus died to make them free. Any believer whose heart is turned toward the Lord will see that what Paul wrote to the church at Corinth can easily be applied to the contemporary church of today.

Secondly, "...the church is out of order..."

The scriptural pattern for the operation of the church in the earth is for the gifts Christ gave us to *"...function..."* according to the purpose for which He gave them. Christ gave *"...apostles, prophets, evangelists, pastors, and teachers..."*, and He gave them responsibility to perfect the saints. According to the Bible these gifts have been given until we all come to the unity of the faith. Certainly, we have not achieved this goal. Most of the church in the earth today doesn't even accept apostles and prophets as viable for the modern day church.

Thirdly, "...the church is complacent..."

Entry level into the kingdom of God is as a babe in Christ. According to our understanding of *"...babies..."* in the natural world, we know that a newborn baby must have constant nutrition about every two to four hours or they will suffer severe consequences, possibly even death. The moment the Holy Spirit inspired use of the term *"...babe..."* to refer to a new believer in the kingdom of God He was giving us the right to use our natural world understanding of a baby to apply to a spiritual baby.

What Peter wrote in his first epistle is so relevant to help us identify the complacency of the church of today:

> *"...as newborn babes, desire the pure milk of the word, that you may grow thereby..."* ***I Peter 2:2***

The expectation of Christ is for a person who is newly born again to desire the pure milk of the word. This desire is to be the same principle desire a natural baby has. A natural baby does not have intellectual understanding of nutrition or any other such knowledge as the basis for desiring to be fed. Intuitively, the baby is simply following his instincts to eat. Perhaps like a natural world bear follows his instincts to hibernate.

So, too, a spiritual babe in Christ has built in spiritual instincts to feast on the word of God as the necessary food with which to live. If a natural baby loses his desire to eat, that loss of appetite becomes a symptom of some possible malady. If the loss of appetite persists for longer than one or two feedings, parents become concerned. Loss of appetite that lasts for a few days typically requires consultation of a physician because the condition is very dangerous and must be properly diagnosed and treated.

The church in the earth today seems to *"...pride..."* itself in losing its appetite. I remember actually hearing a man who had been a believer all of his life tell a new believer who was desperately hungry for more of the Lord that his condition of hunger would pass soon and then he would be like all the rest of the believers. The man giving this hideous counsel even laughed as he gave his counsel to the new believer.

Believers growing in the knowledge of their God do not *"...lose..."* their appetite for God. Their appetite increases more and more because as they grow they learn a principle of growth, revealed by Jesus Himself:

The Expectations of Christ

"...this is eternal life, that they may know You, the only true God, and Jesus Christ whom You have sent..."
John 17:3

Believers growing in the knowledge of their God learn that the more they know their God, the more lifelike He has they too will have!

Jesus identified the priority for our lives. He said,

"...seek first the kingdom of God and His righteousness, and all these things shall be added to you..."
Matthew 6:33

Jesus taught a really important lesson regarding this priority in the principle of asking, seeking, and knocking.

"So I say to you, ask, and it will be given to you; seek, and you will find; knock, and it will be opened to you. For everyone who asks receives, and he who seeks finds, and to him who knocks it will be opened..." **Luke 11:9,10**

Asking, seeking, and knocking is to be a way of life for all believers. When we stop asking, we stop receiving. When we stop seeking, we stop finding. When we stop knocking, doors stop being opened. If the church in the earth today was asking, seeking, and knocking as Jesus instructed, we would all be receiving, finding, and doors opening to us. The church would be full of what believers were receiving, finding, and doors opening from heaven.

These three conditions, divided, out of order, and complacent are where the church is today!

The Expectations of Christ

In order to sustain the simplicity that God has designed in Christ our considerations regarding Christ's expectations for the church need to remain few and *"...simple...".*

1. Jesus must be Lord over the entire church!

Jesus must be Lord at the local level, at the universal level, at any level that can be identified as the church.

2. We must no longer see ourselves as mere men!

We must see ourselves as new creatures, as spiritual men, as the "...body..." of Christ.

3. Jesus must have the preeminence over all!

Absolutely nothing can rise above Jesus as the way, the truth, and the life.

4. We must have no divisions among us!

Believers, as the church, the body of Christ, must all speak the same thing, must have no divisions among us, must be perfectly joined together in the same mind and in the same judgment.

These four expectations are what Christ expects of believers now while we live here on earth. They are certainly not all Christ expects of us, however, if we met just these four expectations, we would see radical changes in our individual lives and in our corporate lives.

When division occurred in the church at Jerusalem over the daily distribution to the Grecian and Hebrew widows, it caused dreadful results. When the Lord's solution was found, two supernatural things happened: The enemy's device of division was removed, and there was great increase in the church.

"Then the word of God spread, and the number of the disciples multiplied greatly in Jerusalem, and a great many of the priests were obedient to the faith."
Acts 6:7

The word of God was spreading, the number of the disciples were multiplying greatly, and a great many of the priests were being obedient to the faith. Were these supernatural events simply coincidental to the Lord's solution being installed in the church? *Were they?!?!* Was God's solution installed to effectually remove the enemy's device of division? *Was it?!?!*

The word, *"...Then..."*, at the beginning of verse seven links the content of verse seven with the previous verses. In the previous verses we are shown there was division in the church; as we have seen causing dreadful results. The installation of the Lord's solution to this need in the church effectually removed division from the midst of the people of God! The division being removed resulted in the word of God spreading, the number of the disciples multiplying greatly, and a great many of the priests being obedient to the faith. It is just remarkable at how destructive the devices of the enemy really are to our lives.

Any device from the enemy will always produce one of the three results of which Jesus spoke concerning the enemy:

*"The thief does not come except
to steal, and to kill, and to destroy."* **John 10:10**

I believe we are going to be greatly dismayed and somewhat overwhelmed when we see the extent to which the enemy has inserted his devices into the church. And how ignorant of his devices we have been so that we have actually yielded to them thinking that is just the way things are, or worse, they are the way we are designed to live.

How Do We Get There?

The very first thing we must do is to change our perspective. If God wills a thing, it is possible for us to do the thing He wills! The church has been deceived by the subtle craftiness of the enemy to believe that God's will is just an *"...ideal..."* to help guide us while we live down here on earth. All of the *"...miracles..."* Jesus did during His earthly ministry really happened. Testimony of them in the Bible was not given to serve as allegories representing some abstract or spiritual meaning. No, testimony of the miracles of Jesus' ministry were given to help us see the profound love and character the Father has toward mankind. Jesus said everything He did was to testify of the Father.

When scripture tells us the Father made Jesus to be Head over all things to the church, which is His body, it means exactly that. Jesus is not to be the Head in name only; He is to be the Head practically. James wrote by inspiration of God the Holy Spirit that we ought not even to make business decisions without consultation and approval of the Lord to determine if it is His will for us to do them.

> *"Come now, you who say, "Today or tomorrow we will go to such and such a city, spend a year there, buy and sell, and make a profit"; whereas you do not know what will happen tomorrow. For what is your life? It is even a vapor that appears for a little time and then vanishes away. Instead you ought to say, "If the Lord wills, we shall live and do this or that." But now you boast in your arrogance. All such boasting is evil. Therefore, to him who knows to do good and does not do it, to him it is sin."* **James 4:13-17**

The subtle craftiness of the enemy is so entrenched in the church in the earth today that we have compartmentalized our lives in Christ into two distinct compartments: our natural lives and our spiritual lives. This compartmentalization leads us to the false conclusion that we are in charge of our natural lives, and we need only consider Jesus' will for our spiritual lives. James called this arrogance and evil.

15

We must change our perspectives to see that Jesus is really to be our Lord, and He really means for His will for the church to be done by the church.

As long as we see God's will from man's perspective we will always fall short of Christ's expectations. Man's abilities have proven to be inadequate. That is why Jesus needed to come to the earth to install a new covenant, a covenant re-uniting God and man once again. This union between God and man would serve as the means for the power of God to flow through the church to accomplish the whole will of God. If we ever hope to meet Christ's expectations for our individual lives and for our corporate lives, this must be the place of our beginning!

Chapter Two

JESUS MUST BE LORD

"...let all the house of Israel know assuredly that God has made this Jesus, whom you crucified, both Lord (2962) and Christ..." Acts 2:36

2962 kurios from kuros (*supremacy*); supreme in authority, i.e. (as noun) *controller*; by impl. *Mr.* (as respectful title): -- God, Lord, master, Sir.

In Paul's letter to the church at Ephesus he writes concerning the Father's appointment of Jesus to various positions.

"Therefore I also, after I heard of your faith in the Lord Jesus and your love for all the saints, do not cease to give thanks for you, making mention of you in my prayers; that the God of our Lord Jesus Christ, the Father of glory, may give to you the spirit of wisdom and revelation in the knowledge of Him, the eyes of your understanding being enlightened; that you may know what is the hope of your calling, what are the riches of the glory of His inheritance in the saints, and what is the exceeding greatness of His power toward us who believe, according to the working of His mighty power which He worked in Christ when He raised Him from the dead and seated Him at His right hand in the heavenly places, far above all principality and power and might and dominion, and every name that is named, not only in this age but also in that which is to come. And He put all things under His feet, and gave Him to be head over all things to the church, which is His body, the fullness of Him who fills all in all." Ephesians 1:15-23

The Church

It is of great importance that we understand Jesus did not *"...take..."* the positions He now holds, they were *"...given..."* to Him by the Father. This has such a place of significance to us because Jesus is the pattern for our lives. Whatever position we are to have in the church, the body of Christ, we must have because it has been given to us, not because we have taken it.

If we used the components of meaning for the term *"...Lord..."* instead of simply using the term itself, it would look like this: Instead of saying, *"...Lord Jesus...",* we would say, *"...Jesus the one who is supreme in authority...".* Use of the single term Lord added to Jesus' name has become little more than an additional part of His name. Lord is not part of Jesus' name; it is the function He has been given over the church. It pleased God the Father when He raised Jesus from the dead to place Jesus as supreme in authority over the church. What a difference between supreme in authority and simply an extension of the name Jesus.

Perhaps if we could get everyone who uses the term Lord as a name to begin using the components of meaning for the term Lord, we could start a process helping the church see the functional meaning of the term. Instead of, *"...Praise the Lord...",* it would be, *"...Praise the One who is supreme in authority...".* Instead of asking a person if Jesus is their Lord, we would ask a person if Jesus is supreme in authority over their life. What a difference! Referring back to James' exhortation to the church, it is arrogant and evil not to make Jesus supreme in authority over our lives, even in business decisions.

Our very salvation is predicated on Jesus being Lord of our lives. Tradition and the doctrine of man has corrupted this concept by making Jesus' Lordship primarily apply to our new birth. Surely our acceptance of Jesus to be the Lord of our individual lives is what gives us right of access to new birth. However, Jesus being supreme in authority over our lives is not meant to be limited to a one time experience, even if that experience caused us to be born again. Jesus as supreme in authority over our lives is intended to be the way we live. When we were born again, we were baptized into Christ becoming a flesh and bone part of His body with Him as the Head.

Using our understanding of a natural body we know the body parts do not move independently of the head, unless there is some neurological abnormality involved. A normal healthy natural body moves in response to the initiative of the head. So, too, the spiritual body of Christ is intended to move in response to the initiative of Christ as the Head. We are designed to live and move and have our being in Him.

"...in Him we live and move and have our being..." Acts 17:28

Jesus being preeminent over all things to the church simply means that nothing has a right to exalt itself or be exalted above Jesus. Because the church is Jesus' body, every facet of the church is His. Every born again believer which comprises every single flesh and bone part of His body was paid for by Jesus' blood!

The Church

"...do you not know that your body is the temple of the Holy Spirit who is in you, whom you have from God, and you are not your own? For you were bought at a price; therefore glorify God in your body and in your spirit, which are God's." **I Corinthians 6:19-20**

"...knowing that you were not redeemed with corruptible things, like silver or gold, from your aimless conduct received by tradition from your fathers, but with the precious blood of Christ, as of a lamb without blemish and without spot..." **I Peter 1:18,19**

Right of ownership of the church in the earth belongs to Jesus! Right to be supreme in authority over the church is His by divine appointment!

In a portion of scripture recorded by Matthew Jesus was issuing a blistering rebuke to the Pharisees. Jesus spoke a decisive word within this rebuke regarding from where the words of a person's mouth originate:

"...out of the abundance of the heart the mouth speaks..."
Matthew 12:34

Anything a person speaks out of their mouth actually comes out of their heart. Whenever a person, such as a ministry gift, takes ownership of the people of God by calling them *"...my people..."*, that person has allowed a subtle device of the enemy to enter as a result of the corruption that is in their own heart. Jesus is very jealous over us. We are all His people. No man has right of ownership or co-ownership over any of us.

This corruptive device from the enemy is not merely a superficial issue, it goes so deep it extends to the operation of the church, the people of God. If any person at any level begins to think for any reason they share in ownership of the people who belong to God, many corruptions will follow. Perhaps the most significant corruption to follow is a change in the *"...way..."* the church operates in the earth.

The three most predominant areas in which the enemy has been most interested in making change in the church are ***government, relationship, and commission.*** The moment a person enters a co-owner role he becomes a captive of the enemy. The enemy begins to infuse corruption into the presumed co-owner, giving him subtle rights to make changes to the design of the Lord for the operation of the church in the earth.

If the enemy can introduce changes to the ***governmental order*** *Jesus has ordained for the church, then it will be easy to change anything he so desires because Jesus will no longer be supreme in authority over the church.* That position of authority will be shared with whomsoever has *"...assumed..."* a co-owner role. Even if Jesus speaks a revelatory word to the local church regarding His way for it to operate, under these conditions two English words will be uttered, becoming the two most malignant words in the English language in the church; *"Yes, but...!"*

For example, a minister brings a revelatory word that Jesus has given five gifts of ministry to us to fulfill the Lord's very specific purposes within the church. This revelatory word even has Holy Spirit inspired scripture already written in the Bible supporting Jesus' giving of these gifts and their purposes. The presumed co-owner hears the word of the Lord, reads the supporting scripture, but then without any grounds to do so, says, "*Yes, but...two of those five gifts are no longer for today.*"

These two words just became radical cells looking to attach themselves to any host that would receive them. The moment any part of the body allows these radical cells, "*...yes, but...*", to attach, a dreadful disease begins to ravage the church: The supreme authority of Christ over the church is reduced.

Government is a topic which has been corrupted by the subtle devices of the enemy in the church in the earth to-day. Even to consider the concept of "*...governmental order...*" causes fear and resistance. However, man did not design the church; God did! Instead of looking at the church from man's perspective, which will always produce an undesirable result, we must begin to view the church from God's perspective. Governmental order is part of God's design for the church.

Jesus the one in supreme authority has given gifts to us. Scripture is absolutely clear in the simplest most direct terms possible "*...who...*" has given the gifts and "*...why...*" they have been given.

> "*And He (contextually can only be Jesus) gave some, apostles; and some, prophets; and some, evangelists; and some, pastors and teachers. For the perfecting of the saints, for the work of the ministry, for the edifying of the body of Christ...*" **Ephesians 4:11,12 KJV**

And scripture is absolutely clear in the simplest most direct terms possible for *"...how long..."* these gifts have been given.

> *"...till we all come into the unity of the faith, and of the knowledge of the Son of God, unto a perfect man, unto the measure of the stature of the fulness of Christ; That we henceforth be no more children, tossed to and fro, and carried about with every wind of doctrine, by the sleight of men, and cunning craftiness, whereby they lie in wait to deceive; But speaking the truth in love, may grow up into him in all things which is the head, even Christ; From whom the whole body fitly joined together and compacted by that which every joint supplieth, according to the effectual working in the measure of every part, maketh increase of the body unto the edifying of itself in love..."* **Ephesians 4:13-16 KJV**

It would be really, really hard for a person to reject the simple terms written in scripture regarding who has given the gifts, what the gifts are, the purpose of the gifts, and for how long the gifts have been given.

With the two words *"...yes, but..."* loosed in the church it was only a matter of time before these radical cells found a host to receive them. The moment part of the body allowed these radical cells to attach, the dreadful disease reducing the supreme authority of Christ began to ravage the church. That part of the church rejecting the offices Jesus has given to fulfill His purposes in His church may not have understood what they were doing, but they were rejecting Jesus' supreme authority over them. How long do you think it will take the enemy to take full advantage of this reduction of Jesus' supreme authority over their lives?

It is bad enough to reject Jesus' design, but the corruption does not stop there. With this rejection man replaces the design of God with the design of man. This change in the design was allowed to be introduced as a result of the subtle corruption of thought from an individual making it acceptable to refer to His people, as *"...my people..."*, His church, as *"...my church..."*, hence establishing a role of co-ownership with Jesus.

If we see Jesus as supreme in authority over the church and the rightful owner of the church, we would not so easily decide to change His design for His church. However, the moment we think for any reason Jesus is willing to share right of ownership of His church or His people, we make ourselves easy targets for the enemy to work through us. Not under any circumstances for any reason does any man have a co-owner role with Jesus. Once we establish that absolute and irrefutable true right of ownership and supreme authority belongs to Jesus, we will be open for Him to tell us how He designed His church to exist and to function. Jesus must be Lord!

*Jesus being supreme in authority over His own church has determined how **relationships** within His church are to operate.* He is very specific in this matter. The change in relationships He requires begins with new birth. Jesus told Nicodemus we must be born again. Nicodemus demonstrated his ignorance of the things of the spirit by asking how a man when he was old could enter into his mother's womb a second time to be born again. Jesus began to give further explanation, but Nicodemus still did not understand. Even though Jesus was introducing concepts of the new covenant, He gave Nicodemus no quarter. He chided Nicodemus, asking him how he was a leader of the Jews and didn't understand these things.

Contained within the dialogue between Jesus and Nicodemus is a premise so powerful it sets the stage for the remainder of our lives throughout all eternity. Jesus is identifying the change of life from the old covenant to the new covenant. The old covenant was based on natural man and whatever abilities he possessed as such. The new covenant is to be based on the spiritual man and the abilities he will be given by His God.

When Jesus told Nicodemus he must be born again, He was offering Nicodemus a glimpse into the world of the new covenant. Nicodemus, even though clearly open to Jesus, was so dull of seeing and hearing, he could only think with his natural mind. The words *"...born again..."* sent him on a wild ride of his imagination. He thought, "How is that possible? How can a man when he is old be born again? Can he enter his mother's womb when he is old and be born again?" As he thought in his heart, he began to speak out of his mouth saying the very words he was thinking.

Over the years I have felt badly for Nicodemus. Jesus was *"...kinda hard..."* on him. Then I began to see something to which I had been blinded. Jesus chided Nicodemus because Nicodemus was functioning as a teacher of Israel. God expects any person in such a place of leadership to have their heart turned toward the Lord and open for His input. Clearly, Nicodemus neither had his heart turned toward the Lord in his role as a teacher nor was he open for input from the Lord regarding his role to teach the people of God. So Jesus chided him.

The enemy will use this device of substituting natural for spiritual again and again in many different forms against the church. The enemy understands that if we ever see the vast difference in quality and power between our natural man versus our spiritual man, we will never be the same. He understands the only way he can rule over us is if we continue to live our lives as mere men here on the earth.

The church at Corinth saw themselves as mere men releasing division in their midst. The church at Galatia was bewitched into thinking that having begun in the spirit they would shift back to the old to be made perfect by the flesh. The strength of the new covenant is based on our change from the flesh to the spirit, from natural man to spiritual man.

"There is therefore now no condemnation to those who are in Christ Jesus, who do not walk according to the flesh, but according to the spirit. For the law of the spirit of life in Christ Jesus has made me free from the law of sin and death. For what the law could not do in that it was weak through the flesh, God did by sending His own Son in the likeness of sinful flesh, on account of sin: He condemned sin in the flesh, that the righteous requirement of the law might be fulfilled in us who do not walk according to the flesh but according to the spirit. For those who live according to the flesh set their minds on the things of the flesh, but those who live according

to the spirit, the things of the spirit. For to be carnally minded is death, but to be spiritually minded is life and peace..." **Romans 8:1-ff**

Jesus as supreme in authority requires that relationships within the church be spiritual, new creature based, rather than natural, mere man based. If for any reason we reject this expectation or think it is impossible to do, we will be rejecting Jesus as supreme in authority. This rejection will inevitably create a substitute for Jesus' expectations; the doctrine of man. This is bad, but this is where the church seems to be living as a way of life today! The same symptoms the church at Corinth were suffering are in place in the church on the earth today.

"...For where there are envy, strife, and divisions among you, are you not carnal and behaving like mere men?..."
I Corinthians 3:3

Absolutely every facet of the church and its successful operation depends on our seeing ourselves as spiritual new creatures, rather than as mere men. There can be no deviation from this, or we will open the door to the enemy to have access to our individual lives and to our corporate lives. Jesus must be Lord!

*Jesus appointed by His Father to be supreme in authority over the church, which is His body, was also **commissioned** by His Father.* Without understanding the commission of Christ, it will be impossible to understand our commission as His flesh and bone body, the church.

When God the Father sent Jesus into the earth, the commission He gave His son was more comprehensive than for Him to just shed His blood as the price of redemption for all mankind. The Father commissioned Jesus to build the Temple of the Lord. *(See Zechariah 6:12, Isaiah 11:1, and I Corinthians 1:30 as scripture references to Jesus' commissioning.)* This unfulfilled commission is also the commission of the church as the flesh and bone body of the Christ.

In order for Jesus and His body to successfully fulfill this commission, the church must...

1. *...understand the commission,*

2. *...have supernatural personnel with divinely given abilities,*

3. *...have adequate provision of material and funds.*

The commission to build the Temple of the Lord is the most comprehensive building project ever undertaken. It involves all mankind who has in the past or who will in the future respond to the call to salvation. Every individual who accepts the call becomes a temple of the Lord the moment he believes and is born again. As temples each believer must undergo construction to be perfected into the image of Christ. Not only is each believer a temple of the Lord, they are each also living stones. As living stones each must be fitly joined together to form the corporate Temple. Building the Temple of the Lord, individually and corporately, is the commission of Christ and His body!

Every member of Christ's body is a supernatural part designed to help fulfill the commission. However, God has given, through Christ Jesus, supernatural personnel to oversee the perfecting of the saints and the building of the Temple. The supernatural personnel needed to oversee successful fulfillment of the commission are apostles, prophets, evangelists, pastors, and teachers.

God supplies each individual believer's need according to His riches in glory by Christ Jesus. He then asks each individual to be responsible for funding His work on the earth. Just as we saw the unchanging God ask the Israelites to be responsible to fund the building of the tabernacle in Moses' commission *(Exodus 25:1-9)*,

> *"Then the Lord spoke to Moses, saying: "Speak to the children of Israel, that they bring Me an offering. From everyone who gives it willingly with his heart you shall take My offering...And let them make Me a sanctuary, that I may dwell among them." Exodus 25:1,2,8*

This same God has asked the church to be responsible for funding the building of the temple in Jesus' commission. We are not to give out of necessity or duty, but out of a cheerful glad heart. We can give cheerfully and gladly because our needs have been met supernaturally by God and because we understand fulfillment of the commission will cause God to manifest His life, nature, and ability within and through the Temple to all mankind.

In order to make these requirements for success work, we must focus on individuals in the church. We cannot be so corporate goal minded that we lose sight of the individual's need and value within the church. Each individual's success in Christ bolsters the success of the corporate church.

Chapter Three

WE MUST SEE
OURSELVES CORRECTLY

The journey of our lives originates within our heart.

> *"Keep your heart with all diligence, for out of it spring the issues of life.* **Proverbs 4:23**

> *"A man's heart plans his way, but the Lord directs his steps..."* **Proverbs 16:9**

> *"...as he (a man) thinks in his heart, so is he..."*
> **Proverbs 23:7**

> *"A good man out of the good treasure of his heart brings forth good; and an evil man out of the evil treasure of his heart brings forth evil. For out of the abundance of the heart his mouth speaks."* **Luke 6:45**

> *"...where your treasure is, there your heart will be also..."* **Luke 12:34**

> *"For the word of God is living and powerful, and sharper than any two-edged sword, piercing even to the division of soul and spirit, and of joints and marrow, and is a discerner of the thoughts and intents of the heart..."*
> **Hebrews 4:12**

The very thoughts and intents of man flow out of the abundance of his heart. In order for us to apply this understanding to our lives accurately we need to see how our heart connects with our actions.

The first step toward understanding in this matter will begin by using Jesus' words as recorded by Matthew,

> *"You have heard that it was said to those of old, 'You shall not commit adultery.' But I say to you that whoever looks at a woman to lust (1937) for her has already committed adultery with her in his heart..."*
> **Matthew 5:27,28**

According to Jesus, this *"...lust..."* a man had for a woman was adultery. In order for our understanding of Jesus' words, *"...has already committed adultery with her in his heart..."* to be complete, we must understand Jesus is telling us whether or not the man ever commits the physical act of adultery, it was already considered adultery by God because it was already done in his heart.

What James writes regarding temptation adds to our understanding:

> *"Let no man say when he is tempted, I am tempted of God: for God cannot be tempted with evil, neither tempteth He any man:. But every man is tempted, when he is drawn away by his own lust (1939), and enticed. Then, when lust (1939) has conceived, it bringeth forth sin: and sin, when it finished, bringeth forth death..."*
> **James 1:13-15 KJV**

In this illustration it is possible for the outer natural part of man to lust for a thing that is forbidden by God, but that lust not be counted as sin just because the flesh lusts for it. Jesus' life serves as illustration of this during His own temptation in the wilderness.

> *"Then Jesus, being filled with the Holy Spirit, returned from the Jordan and was led by the Spirit into the wilderness, being **tempted** for forty days by the devil. And in those days He ate nothing, and afterward, when they had ended, He was hungry. And the devil said to Him, "If You are the Son of God, command this stone to become bread." But Jesus answered him, saying, "It is written, 'Man shall not live by bread alone, but by every word of God.'"* **Luke 4:1-ff**

The Holy Spirit's leading of Jesus into the wilderness included *"...fasting..."*: That made food forbidden to Him. After fasting forty days Jesus' flesh desired the food that had been forbidden to Him, otherwise, He would not have been *"...in all things...made like His brethren..."* **(Hebrews 1:14-18).**

Just because Jesus was submitted to the will of God in this matter, His internal submission did not stop His external flesh from desiring the food that was forbidden. Luke wrote that after Jesus' forty day fast had ended *"...He was hungry..."*. Hunger is simply Jesus' flesh desiring the food that had been forbidden; that is what made it a temptation.

> *"...each one is tempted when he is drawn away by his own desires (1939) and enticed. Then, when desire (1939) has conceived, it gives birth to sin..."*
> **James 1:14,15**

James writes very clearly that a man can desire a thing, even though forbidden, but his desire does not become sin unless *"...conception..."* takes place. Using our understanding of the natural world, conception in relation to the biology of mankind is the fertilization process leading to pregnancy. This process involves two different parts, a male part and a female part, coming together and becoming one. Applying our natural world understanding of conception to what James has written regarding desire becoming sin then, it takes two of man's parts coming together and becoming one in order for there to be conception.

Jesus' flesh desired what was forbidden, but His heart refused to unite with His fleshly desire. There was no conception in the matter, and therefore, no sin. A man's flesh can desire a thing that is forbidden, but that desire not be counted as sin if the man's heart refuses to unite with the desire of his flesh. No conception, no sin!

Jesus' words regarding a *"...man looking at a woman to lust for her has already committed adultery in his heart..."* is a new covenant concept. As a new covenant concept it must align with James' new covenant understanding of conception. In order for the desires of a person to be counted as sin there must be conception present. If a man looking at a woman to lust for her is counted as sin, then the desires of the man's flesh and his heart had to have already united to become one in their desire for the woman. The moment the two parts united together conception took place and sin was produced. ***Conception is required in order to produce sin in the new covenant.***

Scripture says man is made in the image of our Triune God. Man is made up of three parts, spirit, soul, and body. Although we are made of three parts like our God, scripture teaches the function of our lives is either natural or spiritual. We are either going to live as mere natural men or as spiritual men.

Paul addresses the issues of mere natural man versus spiritual man in the simplest of terms in his letter to the church at Rome.

> *"There is therefore now no condemnation to those who are in Christ Jesus, who do not walk according to the flesh, but according to the Spirit. For the law of the Spirit of life in Christ Jesus has made me free from the law of sin and death. For what the law could not do in that it was weak through the flesh, God did by sending His own Son in the likeness of sinful flesh, on account of sin: He condemned sin in the flesh, that the righteous requirement of the law might be fulfilled in us who do not walk according to the flesh but according to the Spirit. For those who live according to the flesh set their minds on the things of the flesh, but those who live according to the Spirit, the things of the Spirit. For to be carnally minded is death, but to be spiritually minded is life and peace. Because the carnal mind is enmity against God; for it is not subject to the law of God, nor indeed can be."* **Romans 8:1-7**

The Holy Spirit is setting the stage through Paul's writings for us to be able to live in life and peace in Christ as a way of life. Paul contrasts those who live according to the flesh with those who live according to the spirit. The weakness of the old covenant was the flesh of man. The strength of the new covenant is the spirit of man.

In his letter to the church at Corinth Paul identifies the limitations and therefore the dangers of the natural man.

The Church

"...the natural man does not receive the things of the Spirit of God, for they are foolishness to him; nor can he know them, because they are spiritually discerned..."

I Corinthians 2:14

In his letter to the church at Rome Paul wrote,

"...For those who live according to the flesh set their minds on the things of the flesh, but those who live according to the Spirit, the things of the Spirit. For to be carnally minded is death, but to be spiritually minded is life and peace. Because the carnal mind is enmity against God; for it is not subject to the law of God, nor indeed can be..."

Here, the Holy Spirit is revealing a profound truth to us through Paul. He is revealing the lives we are to live in Christ are to be spiritually minded rather than carnally minded. A spiritually minded person desires the things of the spirit. A carnally minded person desires the things of the flesh. This revelation teaches us how the mind is involved with either the flesh or the spirit.

If we live according to the flesh, we will set our minds on the things of the flesh. If we live according to the spirit, we will set our minds on the things of the spirit. Either way, living according to the flesh or living according to the spirit, our minds will align with our choice and conception will take place to produce either carnal minded or spiritual minded. Carnal minded is death, involving sin. Spiritual minded is life and peace, free of sin.

Now, how do we begin to make the correct choice to be spiritually minded instead of carnally minded? And when did we make the choice for the first time? When a person bears witness to another person that Jesus is the means to be saved, there is a powerful presence of the Holy Spirit involved to bear witness that Jesus is the Lord, the Savior.

"...I make known to you that no one speaking by the Spirit of God calls Jesus accursed, and no one can say that Jesus is Lord except by the Holy Spirit..."
I Corinthians 12:3

When the person hearing of Christ receives Him, the Father bestows authority to that person to become a child of God.

"...He (Jesus) came to His own, and His own did not receive Him. But as many as received Him, to them He gave the right (authority 1849) to become children of God, to those who believe in His name who were born, not of blood, nor of the will of the flesh, nor of the will of man, but of God..." **John 1:11-13**

1849 exousia (in the sense of ability); privilege, i.e. (subjectively) force, capacity, competency, freedom, or (objectively) mastery (concretely, magistrate, superhuman, potentate, token of control), delegated influence: -- authority, jurisdiction, liberty, power, right, strength.

This *exousia* contains energy from God Himself. The person who receives this authority from God is actually born of God through the vehicle of this energy. When this person is birthed into the family of God, the Holy Spirit baptizes them into Christ to become a flesh and bone part of Christ's body. Such an experience gives the newly born again person a radical change of life and a sight of Christ as the source of their new life. Jesus becomes Lord *(supreme in authority)* in their life. God endows the person entering into relationship with Him certain divine abilities necessary for him to live in Christ. All of this first happens at the time of new birth.

Present within this new believer is an innate hunger for God, just like the innate hunger which exists in a newborn natural infant. The babe in Christ must simply respond to this hunger...

> *"...as newborn babes, desire the pure milk of the word, that you may grow thereby..."* **I Peter 2:2**

As each new born babe in Christ is fed the pure milk of the word, they will grow in their knowledge of Christ. As this knowledge increases, it produces an increase in life like God has in the believer.

> *"...And this is eternal life, that they may know You, the only true God, and Jesus Christ whom You have sent..."*
> **John 17:3**

This spiritual minded desire for God causing us to grow in knowledge and life like God has is to be the pattern for all life in the kingdom of God. It starts at the time of our new birth and is sustained as a result of our continued feeding on and doing the Word of God. This focus on spiritual things starts in the heart, initially promoted by the grace of our God.

Man still has freedom to reject this inspiration to spiritual mindedness, just as Adam had freedom to reject the way of God. Grace offered does not necessarily mean grace received.

Where do our desires originate? Because we are spirit, soul, and body is one of our three parts a *"...desire center..."* where all of our desires originate? Because our mind aligns itself with either our spirit or our flesh, depending on whether we are after the things of the spirit or after the things of the flesh, is our mind the place from which all choices are made? These questions must be answered in order to understand how *"...desire..."* works within us.

Scripture speaks of the *"...desires of your flesh... and of your mind... and of your heart..."*.

> *"And you He made alive, who were dead in trespasses and sins, in which you once walked according to the course of this world, according to the prince of the power of the air, the spirit who now works in the sons of disobedience, among whom also we all once conducted ourselves **in the lusts of our flesh**, fulfilling **the desires of the flesh** and **of the mind**, and were by nature children of wrath, just as the others..."* **Ephesians 2:1-3**

> *"...I say then: Walk in the Spirit, and you shall not fulfill **the lust of the flesh**..."* **Ephesians 5:16**

> *"...Therefore do not let sin reign in **your mortal body**, that you should obey it **in its lusts**..."* **Romans 6:12**

> *"...Delight yourself also in the Lord, and He shall give you the **desires of your heart**..."* **Psalms 37:4**

The flesh, the soul, and the spirit all three can have desires. When you eat your favorite food, the desire of your flesh is satisfied. The desires of your flesh will not be satisfied simply by thinking about a cheeseburger. When you are trying to think a problem through and find an exciting solution, the desire of your soul is satisfied. When you experience the presence of God, the desire of your spirit is satisfied. Certainly an oversimplification, but these thoughts contain a measure of understanding.

Although man is made up of three parts, spirit, soul, and body, scripture has already shown us the function of man is either natural or spiritual. If a man is after the things of the flesh, he will be carnally minded. If a man is after the things of the spirit, he will be spiritually minded. The soul will be aligned with either the flesh or the spirit. Scripture shows us how the soul aligns with the flesh or the spirit. If we live according to the flesh *"...we will set our minds..."* on the things of the flesh. If we live according to the spirit *"...we will set our minds..."* on the things of the spirit.

Man sets his mind either on the flesh or on the spirit.

How is this decision made? Paul's letter to the church at Rome presents a simple but powerful understanding of life from the fall of Adam to life in the new covenant. In chapter six Paul addresses the life a person can have in the new covenant through faith in Jesus Christ. He makes some extraordinary statements about how this new life frees us from the law of sin and death.

SEEING CORRECTLY

"...What shall we say then? Shall we continue in sin that grace may abound? Certainly not! How shall we who died to sin live any longer in it? Or do you not know that as many of us as were baptized into Christ Jesus were baptized into His death? Therefore we were buried with Him through baptism into death, that just as Christ was raised from the dead by the glory of the Father, even so we also should walk in newness of life. For if we have been united together in the likeness of His death, certainly we also shall be in the likeness of His resurrection, knowing this, that our old man was crucified with Him, that the body of sin might be done away with, that we should no longer be slaves of sin. **For he who has died has been freed from sin.** *Now if we died with Christ, we believe that we shall also live with Him, knowing that Christ, having been raised from the dead, dies no more. Death no longer has dominion over Him. For the death that He died, He died to sin once for all; but the life that He lives, He lives to God.* **Likewise you also, reckon yourselves to be dead indeed to sin, but alive to God in Christ Jesus our Lord. Therefore do not let sin reign in your mortal body, that you should obey it in its lusts. And do not present your members as instruments of unrighteousness to sin, but present yourselves to God as being alive from the dead, and your members as instruments of righteousness to God. For sin shall not have dominion over you, for you are not under law but under grace.** *What then? Shall we sin because we are not under law but under grace? Certainly not!* **Do you not know that to whom you present yourselves slaves to obey, you are that one's slaves whom you obey, whether of sin leading to death, or of obedience leading to righteousness?** *But God be thanked that though you were slaves of sin, yet you obeyed from the heart that form of doctrine to which you were delivered. And having been set free from sin, you became slaves of righteousness..."* **Romans 6:1-18**

41

Then in chapter seven Paul starts a transition to contrast freedom in Christ in the new covenant to life back under the old covenant.

> *"...For when we were in the flesh, the sinful passions which were aroused by the law were at work in our members to bear fruit to death. But now we have been delivered from the law, having died to what we were held by, so that we should serve in the newness of the spirit and not in the oldness of the letter..."* **Romans 7:5,6**

Now Paul begins to use his own life to illustrate how he had actually lived under the law.

> *"...What shall we say then? Is the law sin? Certainly not! On the contrary, I would not have known sin except through the law. For I would not have known covetousness unless the law had said, "You shall not covet." But sin, taking opportunity by the commandment, produced in me all manner of evil desire. For apart from the law sin was dead.* **I was alive once without the law, but when the commandment came, sin revived and I died.** *And the commandment, which was to bring life, I found to bring death. For sin, taking occasion by the commandment, deceived me, and by it killed me. Therefore the law is holy, and the commandment holy and just and good. Has then what is good become death to me? Certainly not! But sin, that it might appear sin, was producing death in me through what is good, so that sin through the commandment might become exceedingly sinful.* **For we know that the law is spiritual, but I am carnal, sold under sin.** *For what I am doing, I do not understand. For what I will to do, that I do not practice; but what I hate, that I do. If, then, I do what I will not to do, I agree with the law that it is good. But now,* **it is no longer I who do it, but sin that dwells in me.** *For I*

*know that in me (that is, in my flesh) nothing good dwells;
for to will is present with me, but how to perform what is
good I do not find.* **For the good that I will to do, I do
not do; but the evil I will not to do, that I practice. Now
if I do what I will not to do, it is no longer I who do it,
but sin that dwells in me.** *I find then a law, that evil is
present with me, the one who wills to do good. For I
delight in the law of God according to the inward man.
But I see another law in my members, warring against
the law of my mind, and bringing me into captivity to
the law of sin which is in my members. O wretched man
that I am! Who will deliver me from this body of death?
I thank God—through Jesus Christ our Lord! So then,
with the mind I myself serve the law of God, but with the
flesh the law of sin..."* **Romans 7:7-25**

Paul is not being double minded when he contrasts the truth
regarding life in the new covenant in chapter six with the truth
regarding life in the old covenant in chapter seven.

New Covenant Truth (...in Chapter Six...)	*Old Covenant Truth* (...in Chapter Seven...)
"...he who has died has been freed from sin..." *"...reckon yourselves to be dead indeed to sin, but alive to God in Christ Jesus our Lord..."*	*"...I am carnal, sold under sin..."*
"...do not let sin reign in your mortal body, that you should obey it in its lusts..." *"...sin shall not have dominion over you, for you are not under law but under grace..."*	*"...I delight in the law of God according to the inward man. But I see another law in my members, warring against the law of my mind, and bringing me into captivity to the law of sin which is in my members..."*

43

Paul is merely identifying the amazing deliverance from hopelessly trying to overcome the law of sin and death in your own ability in the old covenant, to the freedom available in the power of God in the new covenant.

To answer the question, *"How is the decision made for man to set his mind on things of the spirit?"*, all we need to do is consider what took place at the time of a person's new birth. One person told another person that Jesus is the means to be saved, and the Holy Spirit manifested Himself in a powerful way to bear witness that Jesus is the Lord, the Savior.

When the person hearing of Christ received Him, the Father bestowed the necessary authority to that person so he could become a child of God. This experience gave the newly born again person a radical change of life, and a sight of Christ as the source of their new life. Jesus became Lord *(supreme in authority)* in their life. God endowed the person entering into relationship with Him certain divine abilities necessary for him to live in Christ. All of this first happened at the time of new birth.

In order for a person to choose carnal mindedness after being born again, they actually have to leave spiritual mindedness. That means they have to lay down what happened to them at the time of their new birth *(even if it is for only a moment)* and replace it with the way of the natural man. Why would anyone do such a thing? The answer holds special significance to any believer who desires to live spiritually minded.

SEEING CORRECTLY

What James wrote to the twelve tribes scattered abroad as brethren gives us the direction needed to begin to answer this question.

"...lay aside all filthiness and overflow of wickedness, and receive with meekness the implanted word, which is able to save your souls. But be doers of the word, and not hearers only, deceiving yourselves. For if anyone is a hearer of the word and not a doer, he is like a man observing his natural face in a mirror; for he observes himself, goes away, and immediately forgets what kind of man he was. But he who looks into the perfect law of liberty and continues in it, and is not a forgetful hearer but a doer of the work, this one will be blessed in what he does..." **James 1:21-25**

The life God gives a person who receives Jesus in order to be born again is amazingly better than the life that person has without Jesus. However, even though this new life is a free gift from God, it must be maintained. The maintenance required is for the new believer to continue in the word and be a doer of the word.

Scripture written by James here is absolutely clear that if a believer does not continue in the word and be a doer, he will be like a man observing his face in a mirror, goes away, and immediately forgets what kind of man he was. Even though the changes wrought in a person's life at the time of his new birth are supernatural and heavenly, the person can and will forget them if he does not continue in the word and be a doer.

Traditional understanding teaches that the pull of the world, the power of the enemy, and the weakness of the flesh are simply too great, and man will eventually succumb to the law of sin and death. Tradition supports this understanding by using Paul's writings to the church at Rome in what we know to be chapter seven. Paul, speaking about himself as an old covenant man before he entered into the new covenant said, *"I want to do good, but no matter how hard I try, I am always pulled away by the desires of my flesh to sin."*

No wonder the church is having such a hard time living as new creatures on the earth. They have been taught it is hopeless to try to overcome sin while living here on earth. It is taught that even Paul the great apostle could not do it. It is absolutely true neither Paul, even though he was an apostle, nor any other man, can overcome sin in the power of his flesh. That is why the old covenant did not produce better results. That is also why God sent His only begotten Son to die for us so we could be redeemed from the law of sin and death. The new and living way is in the power of God given to us at the time of our new birth.

The greater sin is not the sin we committed as an act of the flesh after we had been born again, but rather that we did not maintain the new life God gave us so that we forgot what manner of man we had become! Which do you see as greater, saying a curse word in anger or forgetting what manner of man you had become because you refused to continue in the word and be a doer?

SEEING CORRECTLY

Our God is not angry with us because we have not known or understood the truth about our new birth! He loves us and desires that we live the abundant life He sent His Son Jesus to die to provide us. Turn the past loose! Embrace the joy of a new and living way to live. Our focus is not primarily to overcome sin, but rather to live an abundant life in Christ! Start today by continuing in the word and being a doer!

The Church

Chapter Four

NO DIVISIONS AMONG US

Luke gives account of Jesus casting out a demon. In the account Luke recorded Jesus speaking about the concept of *"...division..."*.

> *"And He was casting out a demon, and it was mute. So it was when the demon had gone out, that the mute spoke; and the multitudes marveled. But some of them said, "He casts out demons by Beelzebub, the ruler of the demons. " Others, testing Him, sought from Him a sign from heaven. But He, knowing their thoughts, said to them: "Every kingdom divided (1266) against itself is brought to desolation, and every city or house divided against itself will not stand. If Satan casts out Satan, he is divided against himself. How then will his kingdom stand? And if I cast out demons by Beelzebub, by whom do your sons cast them out? Therefore they shall be your judges. But if I cast out demons by the Spirit of God, surely the kingdom of God has come upon you. Or how can one enter a strong man's house and plunder his goods, unless he first binds the strong man? And then he will plunder his house. He who is not with Me is against Me, and he who does not gather with Me scatters abroad." Luke 12:22-30*

1266 diamerizo from *1223* and *3307*; to *partition thoroughly* (lit. in distribution, fig. in dissension): -- cloven, divide, part.

Jesus uses the term *"...divided..."* in a very specific manner. His use of the term here is in reference to any kingdom, city, or house that is divided *"...against itself..."*.

In the same letter Luke recorded Jesus using the same term in a completely different manner. Luke wrote:

> *"I came to send fire on the earth, and how I wish it were already kindled! But I have a baptism to be baptized with, and how distressed I am till it is accomplished! Do you suppose that I came to give peace on earth? I tell you, not at all, but rather division. For from now on five in one house will be divided (1266): three against two, and two against three. Father will be divided against son and son against father, mother against daughter and daughter against mother, mother-in-law against her daughter-in-law and daughter-in-law against her mother-in-law."* **Luke 12:49-53**

Jesus' use of the term *"...divided..."* *(1266)* in these two different applications gives us an understanding of the concept of *"...division..."* that is extremely important to us. When division exists within a kingdom, a city, or a house so the kingdom, city, or house is divided against itself, destruction of the kingdom, city, or house will follow.

Such would be the case if Jesus had been casting out demons by the power of Beelzebub. Even in such a case we could rejoice for the fall of Satan's kingdom because of the *"...division..."* within it. If division occurs within a household between father and son because of the revelation of Christ, Jesus said He came to bring such division. It is the desire of our God that all men be saved through the revelation of Jesus Christ. However, we know all will not be saved because not all will accept Jesus to be supreme in authority in their lives. If division occurs between a father and his son because one of them desires to have relationship with Jesus and the other does not, such division is inevitable if Jesus is to be preached expecting men to accept Him here on earth.

It does not bring Jesus pleasure when a father and his son are divided within a single family unit. The division is not what Jesus desires. Jesus simply knows that all men are not going to accept His Lordship and when either a son or his father accepts Jesus and the other rejects Jesus, division will occur. All men entering into salvation is what brings Jesus pleasure. As long as Satan is the god of this world Jesus knows salvation is going to divide households.

Unity at all costs is anti-Christ! Whenever conditions exist within an environment where accepting Jesus to be supreme in authority causes division, *"...division..."* is the will of God! The Holy Spirit inspired Paul to write these words to the church at Ephesus:

> *"I, therefore, the prisoner of the Lord, beseech you to walk worthy of the calling with which you were called, with all lowliness and gentleness, with longsuffering, bearing with one another in love, endeavoring to keep the unity of the Spirit in the bond of peace. There is one body and one Sprit, just as you were called in one hope of your calling; one Lord, one faith, one baptism; one God and Father of all, who is above all, and through all, and in you all..."* **Ephesians 4:1-6**

Absolutely everything within the church, the body of Christ requires the preeminence of Jesus as Lord. Anything that challenges or threatens Jesus' role as supreme in authority over the church is *"...never..."* the will of God!

Believers can say they accept a particular revelation as from God but reject the application of it. The Holy Spirit showed me the error of this way of thinking. He showed me that if believers truly accepted revelation from God in faith, they would also see the value and purpose of the revelation and easily be willing to apply it. Any revelation from God is valuable. He provides us with revelation knowledge of Himself so that we may have life like He has it. So how could a believer accept the revelation God Himself is giving but reject the application of that revelation?

Rejecting application of a revelation from God could take one of two forms, as the revelation applies to others or as it applies to your own life. Either form of rejection could be done actively by choice, or passively by simply not being a doer. James addresses these issues in his discussion regarding faith and works. He wrote:

> "What does it profit, my brethren, if someone says he has faith but does not have works? Can faith save him? If a brother or sister is naked and destitute of daily food, and one of you says to them, "Depart in peace, be warmed and filled," but you do not give them the things which are needed for the body, what does it profit? Thus also faith by itself, if it does not have works, is dead. But someone will say, "You have faith, and I have works." Show me your faith without your works, and I will show you my faith by my works. You believe that there is one God. You do well. Even the demons believe and tremble! But do you want to know, O foolish man, that faith without works is dead? Was not Abraham our father justified by works when he offered Isaac his son on the altar? Do you see that faith was working together with

his works, and by works faith was made perfect (complete)? And the scripture was fulfilled which says, "Abraham believed God, and it was accounted (credited) to him for righteousness." And he was called the friend of God. You see then that a man is justified by works, and not by faith only. Likewise, was not Rahab the harlot also justified by works when she received the messengers and sent them out another way? For as the body without the spirit is dead, so faith without works is dead also." James 2:14-26

According to the Holy Spirit inspired understanding James gives us, a person can believe but have no works demonstrating what they believe. He writes that such believing is *"...doing well..."*, but then, he compares these actions to demons who *"...believe and tremble..."*.

God designed the church to operate with faith and works functioning as a tandem. One of them alone will not produce the desired result: Faith alone will not save you. Works without faith will not save you. God's way is for faith, accompanied by works, to save you! This is the will and the way of God! God's way is simple and easily able to be seen.

How, then, can anyone simply decide that it is alright to believe a particular revelation from God but reject the application of it, either actively or passively? Where does such *"...doctrine..."* originate? And how is it establish within the church? This doctrine is established in layers, so our answers to these questions need to come in layers to create the necessary understanding required to tear down the *"...faith without works is acceptable..."* lifestyle affecting so many believers.

We turn again to James' writings to obtain our first layer of understanding.

"...be doers of the word, and not hearers only, deceiving (3884) yourselves..." **James 1:22**

3884 paralogizomai from *3844* and *3049*; to misreckon, i.e. delude: -- beguile, deceive.

Strong's Exhaustive Concordance of The Bible

deceive

1. to mislead by a false appearance or statement; delude.
2. to be unfaithful to
4. to mislead or falsely persuade others; practice deceit; an engaging manner that easily deceives.

Dictionary.com

According to James' writings the first layer of the doctrine *"...faith without works is acceptable..."* is set in place by the individual believer himself. Any believer who hears the word only and is not a doer, *"...deceives..."* himself. Drawing from the definition provided by **Dictionary.com** helps us see what actually happens within a believer who hears only but is not a doer; such a believer *"...falsely persuades himself..."* that it is acceptable to be a hearer only, and not a doer.

*Persons who hear the word only,
but are not doers deceive themselves!*

The reasons why an individual believer is not a doer are many and varied, ranging from procrastination to rebellion. However, once *"...self-deception..."* is in place a door is opened to the enemy. When the enemy becomes involved, his subtle craftiness begins to add small layers that will ultimately form a huge *"...division..."* within the church.

Layer upon layer from the enemy is established in the church so subtly it is almost impossible to see the devices of the enemy are involved. Jesus is not removed as supreme in authority over the church in a coup; believers would never do that. However, the effects are the same: Jesus no longer has functional direction over the church. If the church is ever going to fulfill its destiny in the earth, Jesus must be Lord over the church. Simply saying or even believing Jesus is Lord is not enough. Faith without works is dead! If we believe Jesus is supreme in authority over the church, we must begin to *"...do..."* what He instructs us to do.

Scripture is very clear concerning the expectations of the Lord regarding divisions.

> *"Now, I plead with you, brethren, by the name of our Lord Jesus Christ, that you all speak the same thing, and that there be no divisions (schisms or dissensions) among you, but that you be perfectly joined together in the same mind and in the same judgment."*
>
> **I Corinthians 1:10**

While there are many *"...reasons..."* believers use to explain away these expectations from the Lord, the most acceptable reason is, *"Well, it is impossible to agree on everything. Let's just agree on the major things."* The Holy Spirit inspired Paul to write *"...that there be **no divisions** among you..."*.

The wisdom and mind of God says,

"Can two walk together, except they be agreed?" **Amos 3:3**

We have already read the words of Christ Jesus recorded by Luke regarding the **consequences** of division...

"...Every kingdom divided against itself is brought to desolation, and every city or house divided against itself will not stand..."

If there are things upon which we cannot agree, we must determine if they are things upon which we even need to agree. Personal preferences such as foods, colors, hobbies, and the like do not fall into the category of things upon which we must agree. However, if there is some doctrinal practice inside the church within which Jesus is designed to have supreme authority, we need to establish agreement so that there be...

"...no divisions among us..."!

SUMMARY & CONCLUSION

The Greek term *"...ekklesia..."* from which the English term *"...church..."* is translated is and was used in a non-Christian manner among Greek speaking people. The term is defined in **Strong's Exhaustive Concordance of the Bible** as:

> *1577 ekklesia* from a comp. of *1537* and a der. of *2564*; a *calling out*, e.e. (concr.) a popular *meeting*, espec. a religious *congregation* (Jewish *synagogue*, or Chr. community of members on earth or saints in heaven or both): -- assembly, church.

According to W.E. Vine's **Expository Dictionary of New Testament Words** the term was...

> "...used among the Greeks of a body of citizens gathered to discuss the affairs of State, *Acts 19:39*. In the Septuagint *(a pre-Christian translation of the Hebrew Bible and some related texts into Koine Greek)*, it is used to designate the gathering of Israel, summoned for any definite purpose, or a gathering regarded as representative of the whole nation. In *Acts 7:38* it is used of Israel; in *Acts 19:32,41*, of a riotous mob. It has two applications to companies of Christians, (a) to the whole company of the redeemed throughout the present era..., (b) in the singular number to a company consisting of professed believers, and in the plural, with reference to churches in a district..."

With such a wide range of uses we need a more precise understanding of the term as it applies to Christians.

SUMMARY & CONCLUSION

The term "...*church*..." has evolved in our vocabulary as a very simple thing to define: *It has come to mean the place a believer goes to fellowship with other believers on a regular basis.* However, the evolutionary process of the term produces an oversimplification which does not conform to scripture. It seems that many terms follow this evolutionary process leading us to false conclusions, as we have already considered the term "...*lord*..." evolving into merely an extension of Jesus' name. What a wrong conclusion this evolution has produced.

According to scripture the church is a great mystery!

> "...*No one ever hated his own flesh, but nourishes and cherishes it, just as the Lord does the church. For we are members of His body, of His flesh and of His bones. For this reason a man shall leave his father and mother and be joined to his wife, and the two shall become one flesh. This is a great mystery (3466), but I speak concerning Christ and the church...*" **Entire context found in Ephesians 5:22-33**

> *3466 musterion* from a der. of *muo* (to shut the mouth); a secret or "mystery" (through the idea of silence by initiation into religious rites): -- mystery.

The simplest route to behold the church as a "...*great mystery*..." is to consider it as the flesh and bone body of Christ. The church is organic, a living being, not an organization.

Although many may not understand what happened to them when they were born-again, every person who was born-again became a flesh and bone part of Christ's body. If a person is not taught properly about their new role in relation to Jesus after new birth, the concept of church that is most widely accepted in our society today will infiltrate the person's understanding, and they will simply begin to consider church as the place they go on Sunday. This certainly must be considered in order for us to properly diagnose *Where We Are* so that we may be able to chart a course *Where We Need To Go*, and *How To Get There*.

We must adopt the way of the Lord to be able to move from where we are to where He desires us to be. The way of the Lord for moving forward comes from a *"...principle..."* we see regarding salvation.

> *"...Whoever calls on the name of the Lord shall be saved. How then shall they call on Him in whom they have not believed? And how shall they believe in Him of whom they have not heard? And how shall they hear without a preacher? And how shall they preach unless they are sent? ...So then faith comes by hearing, and hearing by the word of God..."* **Romans 10:13-17**

We cannot expect a people to change if they do not see the need to change. We must help the church begin to understand *"...church..."* is a great mystery, not simply a place we go on Sunday. And, we must help the people see that Jesus as Lord means more than Jesus has two names, it means Jesus is designed to be supreme in authority functioning over our lives while we live here on earth.

SUMMARY & CONCLUSION

The manner in which we reveal the true condition of the church to the church must be done in faith and with great care. Paul discussed the notion of faithfulness and stewardship regarding the role of persons standing in offices of ministry. He wrote:

> "Let no one deceive himself. If anyone among you seems to be wise in this age, let him become a fool that he may become wise. For the wisdom of this world is foolishness with God. For it is written, "He catches the wise in their own craftiness"; and again, "The Lord knows the thoughts of the wise, that they are futile." Therefore let no one boast in men. For all things are yours; whether Paul or Apollos or Cephas, or the world or life or death, or things present or things to come, all are yours. And you are Christ's, and Christ is God's. Let a man so consider us, as servants of Christ, and stewards of the mysteries of God. Moreover it is required in stewards that one be found faithful." **I Corinthians 3:18-4:2**

It is so extremely important that we treat the church with great love and affection as good stewards regarding what they know or what they do not know. We do not want to be pulled by the gravity of the enemy into a role of "...the accuser of the brethren..." toward the sons of God. That role should be exclusively limited to the enemy and his minions.

It is bad enough the sons of God have been deceived by the enemy to believe a lie regarding what the church is and what it means for Jesus to be Lord. The role of gifts of ministry called to lead the sons of God requires us to see our function and treat the sons with great care. The last thing we desire to do is add shame to their deception by making it seem as if they commissioned the condition of the church to be what it is.

We desire to help the church see where we are in relation to Jesus' expectations, where we need to go to meet His expectations, and how to get there. As we answer these questions, we must be constantly vigilant to keep our own motives pure as to why we desire to show the church answers to these questions. Our motives must be to help the church, the sons of God, see so they may be able to move forward in God. There will surely be a certain amount of correction involved in changing courses. A natural parent bringing correction to a child requires care to avoid harming the child. We must apply this same understanding when beginning to speak correction to the sons of God.

Identifying the church as divided, out of order, and complacent does not have to be given as indictments against the church, but rather simple diagnoses of conditions which exist within the church. Our desire is to help the church see the many layers of the enemy's devices that have been installed over the process of generations. Understanding that Jesus must be Lord over the entire church, that we must no longer see ourselves as mere men, that Jesus must have the preeminence over all, and that we must have no divisions among us must be presented as Jesus' loving care for us. His desire is that we live and not die, that we have the means to abound in every area of life. Everything He wills for us is simply His desire for us to move forward into the place of abundant life.

Understanding the way to get to where He has ordained for us to go starts by our simply believing that if He wills a thing, it is possible for us to do the thing He wills. We must change our perspective of His will to see His will from His perspective and not ours. Church, we can see and do His will! Let us begin to labor together for both to be established in all of our lives...